Tiger Sharks

ABDO
Publishing Company

A Buddy Book
by
Julie Murray

VISIT US AT
www.abdopub.com

Published by Buddy Books, an imprint of ABDO Publishing Company, 4940 Viking Drive, Suite 622, Edina, Minnesota 55435. Copyright © 2005 by Abdo Consulting Group, Inc. International copyrights reserved in all countries. No part of this book may be reproduced in any form without written permission from the publisher.

Printed in the United States.

Edited by: Christy DeVillier
Contributing Editors: Matt Ray, Michael P. Goecke
Graphic Design: Maria Hosley
Image Research: Deborah Coldiron
Photographs: Corbis, Corel, Digital Vision, Jeff Rotman Photography

Library of Congress Cataloging-in-Publication Data

Murray, Julie, 1969-
  Tiger sharks / Julie Murray.
      p. cm. — (Animal kingdom)
  Summary: Briefly describes the appearance, habitat, behavior, senses, and life cycle of one of the deadliest sharks in the world.
  Includes bibliographical references (p.) and index.
  ISBN 1-59197-336-8
    1. Tiger shark—Juvenile literature. [1. Tiger shark. 2. Sharks.] I. Title.

QL638.95.C3M87 2003
597.3'4—dc22

                                                              2003056032

Contents

Sharks..4

Tiger Sharks 6

What They Look Like 8

Where They Live 11

Hunting And Eating 12

Deadly Teeth 16

Senses..18

Shark Pups....................................21

Important Words 23

Web Sites 23

Index 24

Sharks

    Sharks have been around for more than 300 million years. These fish swam the seas back when dinosaurs walked the land. Today, there are more than 350 kinds of sharks.

Some fish have bones. Other fish have **cartilage**. Cartilage is softer than bone. It can bend and is lightweight. Sharks have cartilage instead of bones. Other fish with cartilage are skates and rays.

Rays (top), skates (bottom), and sharks (right) have cartilage.

Tiger Sharks

Of all kinds of sharks, tiger sharks are the fourth largest. Many tiger sharks have markings that look like tiger stripes. This is why they are called tiger sharks.

Tiger sharks have tigerlike stripes.

Tiger sharks and other sharks sometimes bite people. They mistake people for seals or turtles. Sharks often let go when they see their mistake. People are not a shark's natural **prey**. Fewer than 100 people suffer from shark bites each year.

What They Look Like

Tiger sharks are big fish. They commonly grow to become about 12 feet (four m) long. Adults weigh about 1,200 pounds (544 kg). The biggest tiger sharks are 18 feet (five m) long and weigh 2,000 pounds (907 kg).

The tiger shark's color is grayish brown. It is white or light yellow on its underside. The tiger shark's stripes fade as it ages.

Tiger sharks have a light-colored underside.

Tiger sharks have a big, square head and a large mouth. All sharks have a strong tail and **fins** for swimming. The fins on a shark's back are called dorsal fins. The shark's side fins are called pectoral fins. Fins help sharks steer themselves.

Sharks use their fins and strong tail for swimming.

Where They Live

Tiger sharks live near all **continents** except Antarctica. They stay in shallow waters near the coast. They also swim out to the deep ocean waters. Tiger sharks live alone unless they are mating.

Some tiger sharks stay in one area for a while. Then, they move on. Other tiger sharks are always moving from place to place. They often travel long distances.

Hunting And Eating

Tiger sharks commonly eat at night. They go closer to the shore to feed. Tiger sharks go back to sea when they are finished eating.

Dolphins are prey for tiger sharks.

Tiger sharks are **predators**. They hunt and eat animals. Tiger sharks eat stingrays, seals, dolphins, and smaller sharks. They also eat animals with shells, such as turtles, crabs, and lobsters.

Tiger sharks hunt and eat stingrays.

Lobsters, crabs, and turtles are food for tiger sharks.

Garbage Eaters

Tiger sharks are known for eating almost anything. They eat many odd things. Some have eaten soda cans, leather boots, birds, or plastic bags. A tiger shark can get rid of these items, too. It can turn its stomach inside out and force out unwanted objects.

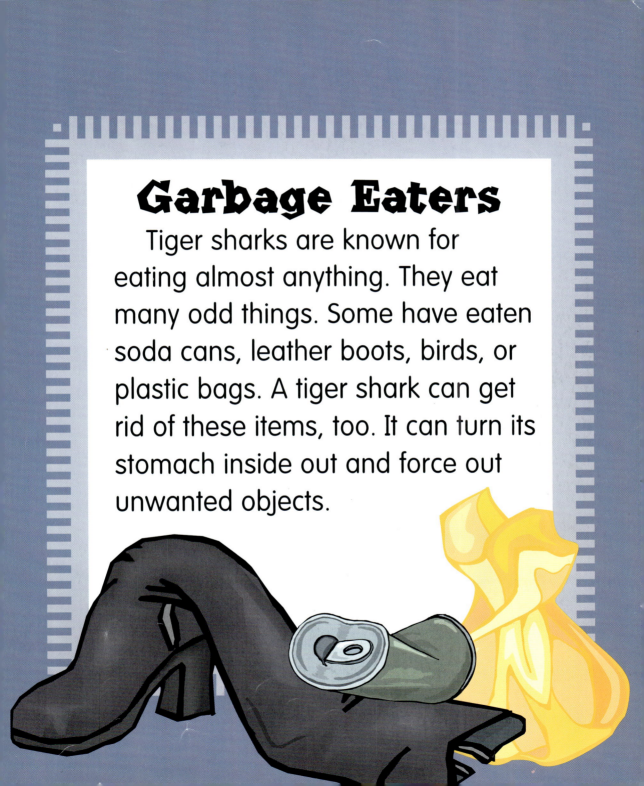

Deadly Teeth

Inside a shark's mouth are many rows of triangle-shaped teeth. Some of the tiger shark's teeth are more than one inch (three cm) long. Each tooth has tiny, sharp points along each side. The shark's sharp teeth can cut very well.

A tiger shark may lose thousands of teeth in its lifetime. When a shark's tooth falls out, another tooth takes its place.

Shark teeth are very sharp.

Senses

Tiger sharks have excellent eyesight. They can see well in dark or murky waters. They also have a good sense of smell. Tiger sharks can smell a drop of blood from 1,300 feet (396 m) away.

Sharks can also sense **electricity**. Tiger sharks can sense the electric field that is around all animals. This helps them find **prey**.

Sharks can sense an animal's electric field.

Sandpaper Skin

Sharks have rough skin. It is full of tiny "skin teeth." These "skin teeth" are denticles. Denticles make the tiger shark's skin very tough. It is hard for other animals to bite through a shark's tough skin.

Sandpaper-like skin around a tiger shark's eye.

Shark Pups

Baby sharks are called pups. Tiger sharks begin life inside eggs. These eggs are inside the mother shark. After hatching, the pups stay inside the mother and grow bigger.

Tiger sharks have between 10 and 80 pups at one time. Newborn pups are between 20 and 30 inches (51 and 76 cm) long.

A young tiger shark

The mother shark leaves her pups as soon as they are born. The pups must take care of themselves. They grow up to become deadly **predators** of the sea. Tiger sharks may live to be 40 years old.

Important Words

cartilage matter that is tough and bendable. A person's ears and nose has cartilage.

continent one of the seven largest landmasses on Earth.

electricity something that happens in nature. Lightning is one form of electricity.

fins flat body parts of fish used for swimming and steering.

predator an animal that hunts and eats other animals.

prey an animal that is food for another animal.

Web Sites

To learn more about tiger sharks, visit ABDO Publishing Company on the World Wide Web. Web sites about tiger sharks are featured on our Book Links page. These links are routinely monitored and updated to provide the most current information available.

www.abdopub.com

Index

Antarctica **11**

birds **15**

blood **18**

cartilage **5**

continents **11**

crabs **13, 14**

denticles **20**

dinosaurs **4**

dolphins **12, 13**

dorsal fins **10**

eggs **21**

electricity **19**

eyesight **18**

head **10**

lobsters **13, 14**

mouth **10, 16**

pectoral fins **10**

predator **13, 22**

prey **7, 12, 19**

pups **21, 22**

rays **5**

seals **7, 13**

skates **5**

smell **18**

stingrays **13**

stomach **15**

tail **10**

teeth **16, 17**

tiger stripes **6, 9**

turtles **7, 13, 14**